I0003452

DeepFake Technology

Complete Guide to Deepfakes, Politics and Social Media

Nobert Young

Table of Contents

Introduction

April 2018 may not be forgotten in a hurry. Jordan Peele is the reason that the date is memorable. This film actor cum producer fabricated a Deepfake content depicting the former president of the United States, Barack Obama, and released it to the public. People who watched the video actually had no idea they were viewing a video engineered by artificial intelligence. They really believed it was Obama until Jordan Peele revealed how he created the footage.

Sometime in May 2019, pictures went viral on the internet showing Mona Lisa with a wide smile which later turned to what looked like a laugh and then silent mouthing of words. This was a cause of concern to many people and this can be explained as a work of Deepfake.

Overtime, we have seen the likes of Mona's portrait as well as Salvador Dali, Marilyn Monroe and several others being used to show the latest Deepfakes technology. Using machine learning, these pictures were depicted as real.

The portraits developed at Samsung's AI lab in Moscow by researchers show an entirely new method of creating real videos from one image. Using few pictures of real faces, the outcome improved dramatically, which birthed what the authors termed "photorealistic talking heads." These researchers also went further to call the result "puppeteering," referring to how invisible strings can manipulate a targeted face. Yes, this can also be used to create your Facebook profile photo.

In the course of this book, we would look at Deepfake and its impact on politics, health, social media as well as its connection to artificial intelligence. We would also talk about how to make a Deepfake video, applications to use as well as how to detect a fake video or picture and so much more.

Chapter One: Deepfakes are Here to Stay

In 2017, a Reddit user under the guise name "Deepfakes" uploaded several videos showing the faces of celebrities like Scarlett Johansson, on the bodies of porn actors. The early examples made use of tools that could place a different face into an existing footage, frame by frame and then this moved on to involve TV personalities and political figures.

What is Deepfakes

Deepfake is a technology that uses Artificial Intelligence to produce or edit contents of a video or an image to show something that never happened.

Deepfakes is a human imaging technology that engages Artificial intelligence for alternating human images. It uses an algorithm referred to as "generative adversarial network" to lay a different photo over the source photo, a process known in the digital graphic world as "Superimposing". In other cases, the photos are not laid over, they are simply combined or mixed. They can be used for either still images or moving images. The word "Deepfake" is an amalgam of two separate words; "Deep learning" and "Fake".

Deepfake employs the use of artificial intelligence for the purpose of engineering realistic-looking fakes. Deepfakes aren't exactly complete fakes if you examine the word critically. They are actually real content that has been doctored and restructured to display something different.

Deepfake is a hybrid of two algorithms; the generator and the discriminator. Their parallel but combined functions have made Deepfake "deep" indeed. The generator is used to create fake video clips while the discriminator is used to determine the originality of the clip. For all the time the discriminator is able to identify the fake, it informs the generator on what to improve to make it hard for the video to be identified as fake.

The easier it becomes for the discriminator to tell the difference between the fake and real thing, the better the generator becomes in trying to produce a fake.

Deepfake is well known in the digital world because it is used to create scandals, wreak havoc and spread malicious agenda. For instance, news can be fabricated using Deepfake and then transmitted to the masses, disseminating falsehood. This technology can be used to cause deception and dent the images of public figures. It is powerful enough to create convincing but false evidence of its victims. Harnessing the destructive power of Deepfakes will not only champion an era of intense misinformation, but it will eventually shift the general audience's impulsive response to information from acceptance to scepticism. Whereas using it for good will boost the sectors of fashion advertising and movie production.

Unlike Photoshop that needs the touch of a seasoned professional before it can bear any resemblance to a real video or image, Deepfakes are quite different because it uses machine learning algorithms. It is easy to detect a fake image or video using Photoshop but with Deepfake, it is not as easy. Deepfakes doesn't need the skill of a seasoned professional to look real, even an amateur can do a good job with it.

This is due to the fact that the software of the app has been programmed to carry out the fakery task. What makes it more deadly is that the main app (FakeApp) is free and readily available for download via the internet.

Deepfakes are dangerous because they are fabricated to be photo-realistic. They make fake look real, a conversion of fiction into fact. This plays on the psyche of people in the sense that the human brain connects what the eyes can see as evidence of something real and true.

The after-effect of this is that there is a general lessening of trust for all videos viewed now because the general public doesn't know what to believe anymore if the videos they watch are real or a perfect fake. Truth is becoming blurry and almost extinct unfortunately.

It is relatively easy once the right tools are in the place for the job. With a good computer system, the software and the information on how to carry out the facial alternations and exchange, as well as the audio simulation, anyone can fabricate realistic-looking content.

Artificial intelligence is the backbone of this technology. It uses tools such as the neural networks which are algorithms. They carry out the fabrication process and they are getting more advanced by the day. Depending on the purpose or intention of whoever is behind a created content, the incredibly powerful technology of the Deepfake can be used for useful applications as well as negative ones.

Historical Development of Deepfake

Scholarly Discovery

Research on Deepfakes was carried out in the sub discipline of "Computer Vision" which is in the Computer Science field. Computer Vision carries out operational procedures in digital visual content i.e. still images and videos. Progress in Deepfake research was made in the year, 1997. This was when the "Video Rewrite Program" announced a breakthrough, showing a manipulated video clip picturing the person uttering the words that belonged to a completely different audio clip. This program also went as far as using machine learning methods such as Speech2Face to sync the facial details with the sounds coming out of the person in the video. That is identifying or unveiling the face behind the voice.

In 2016, Face2Face program, another pet project of Deepfake research, launched a video clip showing a man imitating the facial expressions of another person in reality. The work was attributed to the use of an everyday camera to carry out the technique.

Development by Non-Professionals

Development in this aspect is pioneered in pornography. A well-known Reddit user was known for sharing Deepfake videos alongside other users in the Reddit community. Popular faces were sourced and used to alternate the faces of pornstars in porn clips. The Deepfake technology was also used for non-sexual video clips.

In December, 2017, the world's attention was brought to the presence of Deepfakes being shared as a media content courtesy Samantha Cole's article. She also published another writing saying the number of false pornographic videos manipulated and engineered by Artificial intelligence has significantly increased. This dual publication resulted in the ban of circulated Deepfakes on Reddit communities and other online platforms such as famous social media platform, Twitter and renowned porn site; Porn Hub. This occurred in February, 2018. However, the circulation of Deepfakes continued on other platforms where such regulation wasn't placed.

Chapter Two: The Deepfake Software

Contrary to what some novices think, the application launched with Deepfake capabilities wasn't named "Deepfake". In the month of January, 2018, the FakeApp was invented and released into the market. The basic function of this app was to let people create videos with exchanged or alternated faces, and share these videos as well.

For the fake video to be manufactured, the app employs an "artificial neural network", about 4 gigabytes of space and the graphics processor. For a video containing much data, the app needs a lot of optical data or material to be injected in order to master the aspects of images that needs to be swapped or alternated. It does this by using the "Deep learning" algorithm hinged on the outcome of the video clips and images.

Usually, public figures are the focal point of such videos but less important people are also inserted into the video as well.

Since the advent of the FakeApp, other licensed alternatives have been created, courtesy of the open-source program the forgery application is based on. Using the source code of the FakeApp, similar apps such as Deep Face Lab and Face Swap Live have been invented and launched.

Process of Deep Faking

Making Deepfakes may look like a cumbersome and complex process but it is actually a process with three basic steps. They are the extraction, training and creation. The Face Swap and the FakeApp are the software applications most frequently used to make Deepfakes.

The first step which is the extraction process entails sourcing a lot of data such as pictures and videos possibly thousands of them. Without them, you cannot make a fake video or image. That is what deep learning is all about. Getting injected with so much visual content in order to function on the alternating and swapping.

To streamline the number of contents you want to extract from sources, just get the content featuring the faces and images of those people you want to exchange and that is about it. It is a wonderful short cut to the rather conventional way of extracting both relevant and irrelevant content. When these video clips or images are extracted, their frames will be taken, faces will be distinguished and appropriately positioned. For a face swap to be successful, the measurements of all faces should be identical. Speaking specifically, 256 x 256 pixels.

The second step is the training process. This step basically entails the changing of one face to another. The process employs the use of the neural network to make this possible. The training process is a onetime process but it is a gruelling process that takes multiple hours. This process takes on the initial step of positioning faces and features to be exactly the same before reconstructing.

Creation is the final step in this process. This entails immersing the converted face or image back into the original frame. This seemingly simple process is the most deceptive of all three steps. It is where the Deepfake applications tend to fumble. This is because unlike extraction and training, this step doesn't involve the algorithm. So, the step is error-prone.

Moreover, the frames are done separately leaving little chance for coherence between the different frames and the final video clip comes out with one too many flutters and glitches.

What's Behind the Deepfake technology?

Auto- Encoding

To make a Deepfake video, you cannot overlook auto-encoding. It is a kind of artificial neural network that is used to absorb series of data through a process called unsupervised learning. This process simply involves reducing series of data, then encoding the information for an eventual decoding of the encoded data so that it is close to the source input as it can be. The decompressing abilities of the auto encoder is so because it shuns the "noise" in the data it intends to encode.

Structural make up of an Auto Encoder

The auto encoder is made up of four interconnected parts. They are the encoder, bottleneck, decoder and reconstruction loss.

Encoder: this is where the size of the original input is downsized and encrypted.

Bottleneck: this is where the condensed and encrypted data is at its minimum.

Literally drawing comparisons to contents in an actual bottleneck. It is also where the encrypted input awaits decryption.

Decoder: this is where the condensed data is decoded and modified to be as similar as possible to the original data.

Reconstruction Loss: this process estimates the success of the decryption by the decoder. How much the finished work resembles the original data and the overall performance of the decoder.

Some other classifications of the Auto Encoder are said to be three in number: The input layer, the encoding layer and the decoding layer.

The technology behind deepfaking was designed and manufactured for various intentions. The software was developed for expert use by graphic designers, for leisure use by social media users e.g. Reddit, Twitter and Snapchat. Also designed to entertain people. But it's been used more for negative intentions as opposed to the original intention of the creator.

The movie industry welcomed the invention of the Deepfake initially. Precisely, the alternating of faces which was crucial for some scenes, saved the cost of a stunt double. A good instance is the movie, Rogue One: A Star Wars

Story, which was released in 2016. The makers of the movie used artificial video engineering technology to bring back the character, Grand Moff Tarkin. They did this by simply using the original face of the previous character and superimposed it onto the face of the actor replacing him. This is a good example of an expert use of the Deepfake technology.

A good example of using Deepfake technology for leisure by social media users is the use of face and fun filters on Snapchat. The Snapchat developers keep progressing this technology by repeatedly fine-tuning face detection and tracking so these filters on the app can be more potent.

Apps for Deepfakes

Facial alternations are the trend now that is headlining social media. These are the best apps for swapping faces;

Fake App

This app is well liked by users because it has a user-friendly interface and it is based on the first execution carried out by Reddit user, "Deepfakes".

How to Install the FakeApp

Although the media believes it is easy to create deepfake, however it is not so easy to create a good deepfake. It is not in question that the FakeApp is the most accessible application to create a deepfake. Here you would learn how to install the FakeApp and how to use it.

Like other face-swapping software, FakeApp was built on the implementation provided by the Reddit user "Deepfakes". While we have other softwares like GitHub's Faceswap, Fakeapp remains the best as its easy to use. When downloading any of these softwares, ensure it is from a trusted site to avoid downloading malwares and trojans to your system.

Step 1: Install Nvidia CUDA9

FakeApp makes use of neural networks that are very expensive to train. Regardless of this cost, the process involved in training a neural network is too parallelizable. Due to this, several Machine Learning frameworks like TensorFlow and Keras, make use of GPU (Graphics Processing Unit) to dispatch the computation. GPU is a chip in the computer that processes graphics entries.

The app employs the use of Artificial Intelligence framework "Tensorflow" owned by Google that supports GPU-accelerated computations with NVIDIA graphics cards.

- To start, first install CUDA$^{®}$, a computing software that sends intensive computation to the NVIDIA GPU.

- Next is to check your Graphics Card. Not all NVIDIA card have the needed support for GPU computing. To confirm the compatibility of your GPU, simply visit, CUDA GPUs. Graphics cards with compute capability of 3.0 and above can work. (https://developer.nvidia.com/cuda-gpus).

- Although FakeApp allows you to use your models without the GPU, I would not advise on this as it can take up to weeks for what you can achieve in hours.

- Update your NVIDIA Drivers. Ensure your drivers are updated before you attempt to use CUDA®. Visit NVIDIA Driver Downloads page to carry out the update. (http://www.nvidia.co.uk/Download/index.aspx)

- Install CUDA® Toolkit 9.0. Once you have updated your drivers, visit CUDA® Toolkit Download page to download the correct CUDA® Toolkit. (https://developer.nvidia.com/cuda-90-download-archive)

- It is important to select the right version to match your system OS and CUDA.

- You have the option of choosing your preferred installer type.

- You would get a pop-up on installation, select "Custom" from the list and tick all the components.

- Install cuDNN. The CUDA® only gives you the basic tool needed for GPU computing. You need to download the cuDNN also known as the CUDA® support for "Deep Neural Networks" to give you access to the libraries for specific tasks.

- You need a login to be able to download the cuDNN. First register for free via the NVIDIA Developer option. Then go back to the webpage to get the download link.

- FakeApp is compatible with cuDNN 7. The cuDNN is a zip file that has all the needed libraries. To install, first extract the contents and merge with the CUDS/v9.0 folder in your computer usually (C:\program files\NVIDIA GPU computing Toolkit\CUDA\v9.0).

- Configure the Path System Variables. Fakeapp needs to be granted access to both the cuDNN and the CUDA®. When you install the CUDA9.0, it automatically updates your Path.

- Ensure that the CUDA® updated your path for FakeApp to work.

Step 2: Install the FakeApp

- Visit the FakeApp Download page to download https://www.fakeapp.org/downl oad.

- You would need to download two files. First is the main installer for the FakeApp binaries, the second is the **core.zip** that has all the dependencies for the app. Once you extract the zip, merge all the contents in the C:\Users\[USER]\AppData\Loca l\FakeApp\app-2.2.0\resources\api folder.

- If done correctly, then your FakeApp is ready for use.

How to Use the FakeApp

As explained above, to create deepfake involves three steps: the extraction, training and creation. This would be applied to the FakeApp.

Step 1: Extraction

- FakeApp requires a large number of images to be able to train your model. If you do not have hundreds of pictures ready, FakeApp would give you access to extract all available frames from a video. To do this, simply type in the mp4 video link in the **Get Dataset** Tab, then click on Extract to begin.

- Once the files are extracted, you can delete other files while you keep the extracted folder. Go through the faces to confirm that the faces aligned remain aligned as this can fail sometimes.

- Basically, all you need is two separate videos of 2 persons. Then run the process twice to give you two folders. When you have several videos of one individual, extract all the videos then merge the folders together. On the other hand, you can add the videos together using Movie maker or other similar software.

Step 2: Training

- From your FakeApp, go to the Train Tab.

- Under Data A and Data B, copy out the path for the folders you extracted. Data A has the extracts from the original video while Data B has the images of the individual you want to insert into data A video. In this process, the face of person B would be imposed on that of person A. You would also need a different folder to store the model. In actual fact, the neural network works in both direction and makes no difference which you specify as A or B.

- Set up the training settings before you begin proper. On the screen, you would have the parameters to set. You use the Nodes and Layers to setup the neural network, Batch Size for training larger number of faces.
- Adjust your settings based on the size of your GPU. The below would show you the recommended settings:

Parameter	2 GB	8 GB
Batch Size	16	128
Nodes	64	1024
Layers	3	4

- Without enough space, you would be unable to complete the process.

- Next is to Monitor the progress. During training, a window would appear to show the performance of the neural network. Pressing Q at any time would stop the process. To restart, follow the same folder. FakeApp would also show a score of errors done during the process.

Step 3: Creation

- This process is similar to what obtains in **Get Dataset**. Provide the link to the mp4 video and your model folder. This is the folder that houses the files: endoder.h5, decoder_A.h5, and decoder_B.h5. You should also state the target FPS.

- Once you click on Create, you will have:

- Extraction of frames from the original video in the **workdir-video** folder.

- Cropped and aligned faces in the **workdir-video/extracted** folder.

- This instruction would also process each of the faces using the model trained.

- Merge the faces into the source frame and save them in the **workdir-video/merged** folder.

- The final stage is to add all the frames together to give the final video.

- In the next screen, under Settings, you would see the option to switch from Person A to B or person B to A.

Snapchat

This software makes use of filters to alternate the faces of the user with someone else such as a friend. It goes beyond this, this app also has so many other features, but the most widely used feature is the face swap feature. This app is quite popular and it is available on Google play store and Apple Store. The use of this filter for the face swap doesn't just swap faces with some clicks, it extracts faces from images and it also supports instant sharing of these newly made photos with friends.

How to Face Swap using SnapChat

Face swaps are trending but not everyone knows how to make use of the face swap technique. Here is a guide for those that use Snapchat:

- First of all, install the Snapchat from Apple store or play store if you don't have it already. Make sure it is the most current version.

- Launch the application and make sure it is on selfie mode, ignore the shutter button and hold on to your face on the camera.

- Do that till you see the face map. This means your application lenses are active.

- Navigate across these lenses till you see the Lens for the Face Swap effect. It's represented by a yellow icon with two emoji faces.

- These emoji faces will now show on the screen. Stay close to the person or object you want to exchange faces with.

- Position your faces with the emoji faces, once the faces are properly positioned, they will become yellow on the camera screen. For this to work, don't wear glasses while doing it.

- Once these faces are properly positioned, Snapchat will alternate the faces and whatever expression is on it. Whatever you did with your face will reflect on the other face.

- To save swaps, tap the shutter button at the base of the screen.

Cupace

This app contains photo editing features. It has the ability to superimpose photos via one of its features called "PasteFace". This is possible because this app is capable of manually extracting the complete facial details from images, this is a process that can be carried out on its own even when the user has no intention to actually swap faces.

With Cupace, one can easily remove the face from an image, choose another image and plant it on that image. This app also has magnifying features so you can zoom in the face you intend to swap or plant on another to ensure there is no error in the extraction of the face. Any face removed is stored in the app and can be used for pasting on several faces. This app is available on Google play store.

Face Swap Live

While Snapchat holds the title for the most popular face swapping application, this app holds the title for the being the best in the face swap game. Its features make it possible for you to exchange faces with your friends in real time. This can be done by getting your friend to face the camera frame with you, so the app can exchange your faces in real time. This app does it live while other apps use still images, and this is the edge the Face Swap live have above the others.

The app can record video clips of you with your new face but for all these features to be able to work, the viewfinder of the camera needs two faces staring at it in order to do the job.

It also has filters that photo lovers can use to add fun and swag to their images. This app is exclusively on Apple store for now but the Android version is coming soon.

Face Swap Booth

This app is cool because you can add faces to be used for swaps either manually or automatically via the app. The app comes with already stored images of celebrities. You can make your pick and alternate faces as it suits you. The app has sophisticated tools for editing, face masks and so on. It has a free version and a premium version that you have to pay for be able to add numerous photos, faces, cut out advertisement and watermarks. It is available on both Google play store and Apple store.

Mix Booth

This app performs a different function from the rest. It doesn't alternate faces but it mixes two faces into one. The app enables the user to add images of people he wants his face combined with. Be it a stranger's face or that of a celebrity, your options are limitless.

DeepNude App

This app was banned due to its perverse function. It was capable of creating false, naked images of women whose pictures it captured. It wasn't accessible to Android users, just Windows and Linux. The app just applied to female images. Development was being done for the male version but I doubt that will continue as the app is no longer available.

Chapter Three: Artificial Intelligence; What makes Deepfake Possible!

Artificial Intelligence also known as AI is a branch of computer science that focuses on developing intelligence machines to think and work like humans especially computer systems. Examples of this include problem solving, speech recognition, learning and planning. The process for artificial intelligence includes learning (this is getting the information and rules governing usage of such information), reasoning (making a definite or approximate conclusion from the rules) and self-correction.

Simply put, it is the machine or automated version of the human intelligence and cognitive skills. It can also be regarded as the simulated version of the human intellect and processes involving that intellect. Quantum leaps have been made in the field of computer science, programming and communication thanks to this innovation. By cognition, am referring to the tasks that require intelligence. Tasks such as providing solutions to problems and comprehension.

Artificial intelligence could be strong or weak. Weak or narrow artificial intelligence is developed and programmed for a specific task. This means they cannot operate outside the scope for which it is built. A good example of this is Amazon's Alexa and Apple's Siri, they are smart virtual assistants trained to obey and execute voice commands. Strong artificial intelligence are the ones that carry out general tasks not being limited to a certain type. When it is faced with a task, it doesn't need the input of humans before it can carry it out.

Corporations and individuals now utilize artificial intelligence as a service by testing it in numerous business interests and on different platforms before committing to it. Vendors incorporate artificial intelligence into their standard offerings due to the costliness of the resources, hardware and software for artificial intelligence. Artificial Intelligence cloud offerings that are well known include; Google AI, Amazon AI, Microsoft cognitive services and so on.

When it comes to algorithms for deep learning, their intelligence or learning ability is limited to the data being fed to these algorithms during training.

The components of artificial intelligence include applications, model types, language for building and programming these models, software for training models. Applications include; analysis of sentiment, recognition of speech and image, bots and generation of natural language. Model types; deep learning, machine learning and neural networks. Programming languages such as Python, Java, C and TensorFlow. Software/

hardware for models include graphic processing units, parallel processing tools, cloud data storage and computer systems.

Categories of Artificial Intelligence

Artificial intelligence comes in classifications; analytical, human-inspired and humanised artificial intelligence.

First to understand is the Analytical Artificial Intelligence. This is the cognitive aspect of artificial intelligence. It draws on information culled from last experiences of human beings to analyse and provide decisions for the future.

The next is the Human Inspired Artificial Intelligence. This draws on the traits of both the human cognition and emotions. Decisions are not just reviewed, analysed and given; they are also considered emotionally. This is because artificial intelligence has learnt to comprehend human emotions and incorporate it.

The last category is the Humanised Artificial Intelligence. This is the social aspect of artificial intelligence. It doesn't limit itself there. It carries along cognitive and emotional traits of human intelligence as well. Innovations such as a robotic personal assistant is a good example of the above category. They can interact meaningfully with humans.

Michigan State University scholar, Arend Hintze who is an associate professor of integrative biology and computer science and engineering has his own categorization for artificial intelligence ranging from existent to futuristic systems. His categorisation is as follows;

Reactive Machines

A good example of this is the Deep Blue which is the brainchild of the IBM. It is a chess program that became known when it defeated Garry Kasparov in the 90s. This app was capable of recognizing pieces on the chess board and predicting its next move, but its analysis doesn't stem from past moves or occurrences because it has no information storage facility to retrieve such data. So, it focuses on the present, it's moves and the opponent's move and plays. Another good example is AlphaGo, brainchild of Google. Reactive Machines are built for a particular task and are not flexible enough to be adapted to another task.

Limited Memory Machines

These machines have information storage facilities so they can analyse future decisions and make them based on past occurrences. The observatory abilities of the machine help it make a decision for the near future, such as a self-driven car switching lanes and turning bends. The memory is limited because this information is stored temporarily.

Theory of Mind Machines

This refers to an artificial intelligence that others have their beliefs and purposes and it factors the decisions they make. This is a futuristic category. Such artificial intelligence doesn't exist yet.

Self-Awareness Machines

This refers to a not yet existing model of artificial intelligence that has a self-consciousness and can use information to draw inferences on the emotions of people.

Examples of Artificial Intelligence Technology

Over the years, artificial intelligence has been integrated into various technologies. Some of which will be mentioned and discussed:

Automation

Artificial intelligence is responsible for the automation of machines. Such machines such as Robots can perform human tasks without any assistance from the humans themselves. They can perform a lot of tasks at a much faster speed because they don't experience fatigue and they keep at it repeatedly. If used in a factory, they will increase production output.

Machine Learning

This process refers to the study of triggering a computer into action without having to program it.

It has four subsets. They include:

- **Deep Learning**

This is the birth process for the Deepfake software. It is automatic prediction analysis. It involves artificial intelligence triggering machines to learn how humans learn to gain knowledge and store large volumes of information from which it draws its intelligence.

- **Unsupervised Learning**

Sets of data are not given names and they are categorised according to what they share in common and what they do not.

- **Supervised Learning**

Sets of data are given labels so that patterns among them can be easily noticeable and used to give labels to new sets.

- **Reinforcement Learning**

Just like the unsupervised learning, it doesn't label sets of data but it gives a feedback to the artificial intelligence system after an action or series of actions.

Machine Vision

This is the automated simulation for the human vision but it is more advanced. It is the technology that first of all, involves the capturing then analysing of data with the use of a camera, conversion from analog to digital and then digital processing. It can be used for medical imaging in operating rooms or identifying signatures. It deals with the processing of images.

Robotics

This is an engineering field concerned with the development and creation of robots. They were created to aid humans with stressful tasks or tasks that needs consistence not fatigue to be carried out. They are used for tough tasks such as assembling car parts, sending huge objects into space. Robots are also designed for interactive purposes.

Natural Language Processing (NLP)

This has to do with a computer program processing human language. One common example of this is Spam detection where the system determines if an email is junk by looking at the subject and content of the email. Sentiment analysis, text translation as well as speech recognition are part of tasks included in NLP.

Self- driving Cars

This combines image recognition, computer vision and deep learning to create automated skills to pilot a vehicle while remaining in a specified lane.

Examples of AI technology

AI applications

Artificial intelligence has been used in several areas and below we would give six examples of this:

AI in healthcare:

Companies and health facilities now make use of machine learning for better and accurate diagnoses that cannot be achieved by humans. The aim is to improve patient outcomes while cutting cost. One of the best healthcare technologies in the world today is the **IBM Watson**. This machine not only understand natural languages but also responds to whatever questions are asked. It forms a hypothesis from patient data and other available sources. Other AI applications are chatbots, this is an application that is used online to answer questions and help customers to schedule follow-up appointments as well as help with billing processes and provide basic medical assistance.

AI in business

Tasks that were previously performed by humans are now being carried out by machines through robotic process automation. Machine learning algorithms are being fed into CRM platforms and analytics to give information on improving customer service for businesses. Websites now use the chatbot to provide instant service to their customers without human interference.

AI in Education

With AI, gradings have become automatic, thereby giving educators extra time to focus on other aspects. With AI, students are able to work at their own pace. AI tutors are also available to give extra support to students and ensure they do not go off the track.

AI in Finance

Applications like the Turbo Tax or Mint make use of AI in their application and this has disrupted the financial institutions. These applications spool out customers' personal data which they use to provide expert financial advice. Today, we see applications like IBM Watson being used in purchasing a home. Also, most of the trading done on Wall street are carried out by software.

AI in law

It is most times tiring and cumbersome for lawyers or law professionals to go through several documents before arriving at a conclusion or decision. It is therefore very useful to automate most of these processes. Many start-ups today have built in question and answer assistants in their computers that can sort programmed to answer questions by going through the taxonomy and ontology of a database.

AI in manufacturing

This area has since witnessed the automation of processes. Industrial robots have been employed to perform tasks previously performed by an individual.

The use of artificial intelligence to generate videos and audios that are a result of deep learning from the original content has raised issues of concern and security. The use of advanced artificial intelligence tools to create a content depicting an event or action that never took place is something that surely draws attention.

However, the advent of the Deepfake made possible by the use of artificial intelligence algorithms is neither good nor bad. It's uses and effect solely depends on who has such technology in his or her hands and the intentions behind the use. The unfortunate outcome is that it is more abused and this has tilted this brilliant innovation to the side of negativity.

Background of Artificial Intelligence

Unknown to many who believe Artificial intelligence came out in the 21st century, it actually dates back to an earlier period in history. It began as an academic field in 1956. Its progress has experienced a topsy-turvy flow on its path. It has been through a period of insufficient funding, pessimistic tendencies then bounced back due to adequate funding and novel approaches.

Mathematical equations, search optimization and artificial neural networks are few of the numerous tools that is used by Artificial Intelligence. This sub-discipline in Computer Science, draws energy from renowned disciplines such as Mathematics, Engineering, Philosophy, Information technology, Linguistics, Psychology and so on.

Artificial intelligence was birthed on the basis that a machine can imitate human intelligence. This has sparked some controversy as some ethical questions have been raised about the invention of artificially engineered creatures endowed with simulated human intelligence. Other ethical dilemmas point to its unchecked progressiveness as a threat to the human race most especially in the employment of human resources in factories.

Shortly after the invention of Artificial intelligence, precisely in the mid-1960s, the United States Department of Defence provided heavy funding for further research on the innovation and planted research centres in various locations. However, the optimism of the inventors soon gave way to realism as they figured their speculations won't occur as predicted. Progress halted due to some tasks being difficult for their invention and the British and American government cut short funding for the research.

This was a downtime for the Artificial intelligence project and it went on like that till the 1980s. The project bounced back with a big bang with the success of the Analytical Artificial intelligence. It sold huge on the market. This period of glory didn't last for long as the rainy days came back for the Artificial Intelligence project. In 1987, when demands for the Lisp Machine withered, the Artificial Intelligence research suffered another setback.

In the early 21st century, as processing power for the artificial intelligence increased, its use was now adopted in fields such as logistics, data mining and so on.

2015 in particular was a wonderful year for the progress of artificial intelligence as its use within Google significantly increased as compared to 2012 according to Bloomberg's Jack Clark. Its use was featured in almost three thousand projects. Artificial intelligence is also responsible for the drastic fall in errors related to processing of images since the year 2011.

Another profound example is a system developed by Microsoft to automatically convert one language to another and one developed by Facebook to depict images to people with visual impairments.

Artificial intelligence is founded on a set of programmed instructions that a computer can carry out. These algorithms are programmed to learn from gathered information (deep learning). It is capable of extracting as much knowledge as possible by considering all the possible theories and correspond them to the data extracted. However, not all theories or possibilities are considered of use by Artificial Intelligence. It circumvents the unproductive theories and focuses on the productive ones.

Artificial intelligence as mentioned earlier draws inferences and decisions from a collection of past occurrences, and decide on its earlier success as a likely guarantee for an impending success in future. Decisions are not farfetched; they are mostly ones that are safe from failing. So, it appears that Artificial intelligence is never wrong but its output is limited to its data and inherent ability.

The ultimate intention of the Artificial intelligence invention is to enable computer systems and machineries to operate intelligently. Just like human beings find solution to puzzles and use logic to deduce conclusions from observations, artificial intelligence, due to certain algorithms programmed to mimic these human cognitive functions, can also do the same thing.

Chapter Four: Practical Applications of Deepfakes

Politics

Renowned and accomplished politicians have been misrepresented due to Deepfake videos targeting them. In such videos, they appear to be saying things they actually didn't say. Misrepresentation by the creators of such videos apparently have no limits as it went to the extent of swapping the faces of some of the world's most powerful individuals. For instance, the chancellor of Germany, Angela Merkel had her face alternated with that of the United States President, Donald Trump. Another daring instance was when the face of former Nazi leader and dictator, Adolf Hitler was swapped for that of the Argentine President, Mauricio Macri.

In the month of January, 2019, KCPQ, an affiliate of popular television outfit, Fox television broadcasted Donald Trump during his public address at the oval office, making fun of his outlook and skin tone. The video was manipulated of course, and Donald Trump's facial colour was modified to a deep orange.

As much as these applications of Deepfakes are unsettling in the political arena, politicians can turn around to use this forgery technology for their own benefits as regards electoral campaigns.

Campaigning has always used the media technologies to win the favour of the electorate, and get them to elect their candidate and it seems they will be turning to Deepfake soon as it appears to be the future of political campaigning. A sad speculation.

The Deepfake can be used to give false digital impressions of full crowds and overflow. The ideology is that voters tend to go with the ones who can pull the crowd at rallies because they believe these contestants have what it takes to lead.

Software capable of generating crowds in an auditorium that is actually empty can be used to locate the empty seats and plant synthetic faces designed to match the demographic requirements of the crowd the politician is addressing. The more crowd you can pull, the higher your chances of getting more support. This crowd generation software is powerful enough to not only fill seats, but to also create the impression that there is an overflow of people outside the auditorium.

The deep learning technology doesn't just create digital visuals, it also extends to audio fakery. Artificial intelligence can imitate the voice of whoever you want by generating voice models.

The forgery even extends to post production of the fake video clip.

Credible news broadcasting outfits can air the video feed and show the original video which points out to a half-empty of almost empty stadium but then the politician can always say that clip was recorded before crowd control admitted people in for the rally and then present his own forged video clip showing an overwhelming crowd. The politician can go further to accuse the broadcasting outfit of trying to scandalise him by airing an altered video in which the crowd was removed from the venue of the rally just to discredit his charisma and weaken his morale. He can present himself as a victim of unfair media assault thereby playing the pity card and gaining more supporters.

Apart from using the Deepfake in one's favour to win supporters, it can also be used by desperate politicians to tweak the rallies of opponents who they feel is a threat to their political goals and ambitions. They can use the Deepfake to digitally remove the real crowd in the auditorium and create a synthetic impression of a seemingly empty space and also insert scandalous and negative messages on the placards held by the supporters. All in a bid to reduce the opponent's popularity and sway public favour away from such individual or party.

Another application of the Deepfake in the political sector is forging political advertisement in large numbers, making up information just to sell your ideals to the electorate. Each advertisement campaign is forged with a unique message for a particular sector of the general demographic. The footage of the campaign can be tweaked to reveal the candidate uttering statements already provided by the algorithms of the deep learning technique, and the artificially created audience showing their support for the message and the candidate. The footage can depict the candidate with a signature look and showing the audience with a similar outfit such as a branded t-shirt or a cap. This can extend to real time as you start seeing people who are in support of the candidate start wearing such clothing to advertise their support publicly.

As discussed above, the Deepfake technology can be used to cast a negative light on their opponents and also promote one's political ambitions giving him real life support from real life people. However, it is done through manipulation of visual content meant to look real and convincing.

Pornography

Adult entertainment is unfortunately the area where the Deepfake technology is most frequently applied. Many instances of famous people having their faces swapped or superimposed in fake video clips bringing serious scandals and negative attention to the celebrities.

Fake pornography emerged in 2017 on Reddit precisely. An unknown Reddit user going by the alias "Deepfakes" uploaded quite a number of pornographic videos online. Notorious among them was the "Daisy Ridley" Deepfake. The English actress became an unfortunate victim, and became a prominent feature in several articles for the wrong reasons.

Another infamous instance of Deepfake pornography is the clip of Wonder Woman star, Gal Gadot, depicted having sexual intercourse with her half-brother. The list of Deepfake victims doesn't stop there. It extends to Emma Watson, Scarlett Johansson and so on.

Fortunately, these artificially engineered scandals did not last as they were disproved as forged clips. But then, the Deepfake technology was in its early stages of development so it was still easy for the ordinary eye to look closely and detect the video as a fake. The case is different now. The Deepfake technology has rapidly progressed to an extent that an artificially engineered video clip looks as good as an original and detection of forgery is almost impossible to the naked eye.

Several bugs have been developed and designed for insertion into these doctored footages making it hard to distinguish between a forged video and a real video. Creating a pornographic video using celebrities is pretty easy. Because they are public figures, there are numerous pictures of them online. One can easily access these images during extraction and use them for the exchange and alternation.

Sovereign states such as the United Kingdom has penalised the act of "deepfaking" as harassment in order to combat this digital forgery menace. But that has not aroused sufficient satisfaction and there is a public outcry to make the act a specific crime in the constitution.

In the legislative chamber of the United States, the act has been related to offences like "Cyberstalking", "Identity theft" and "Revenge Porn". But there is still calls for a more complete insertion of the act as an offence on its own.

Complete Body Deepfakes

This aspect of Deepfake is yet to progress to a stage of "almost impossible detection" but it exists already. Not just the face or voice can be engineered but the entire body as well. However, it is easy to detect for now. This forgery was initiated in Heidelberg University and published by GitHub.

This has generated a public dread, for it is more of a glimpse of the future capabilities of this aspect of forgery. Now entire bodies can be alternated and engineered within an artificially created environment. This simulation is carried out by the algorithm. It latches onto your bio information such as an image of you and your body movements. Then within that video setting, you will be engineered to look like you are moving and performing whatever activity the user of such technology deems fit.

For instance, in the sport of lawn tennis, an individual who has no experience with the sport can be simulated and engineered to seem like a seasoned professional in the video clip. With data of human body movements being learnt by Artificial Intelligence, the software can predict your next move and modify the video feed accordingly.

The complete body Deepfake is still sketchy and the glitches in simulation can be the basis for easy detection.

Social Media

Social media platforms are trying to address the distribution networks of Deepfake content. Proposals have been made to make regulations and policies regarding the dismissal of Deepfake from their sites. This issue of policy is more than it seems because its focused on fabricated content will be too generic in its coverage, and will be perceived as an unacceptable policy by users as Deepfake isn't just used negatively only but positively as well. Not all Deepfakes are actually forgery so it will be difficult for social media platforms to enact regulations that are pragmatic, precise and in line with how they address other forms of false content uploaded on social media.

Recently, an engineered video of Mark Zuckerberg uttering apocalyptic statements such as being in control of billions of people's data enables him control the future went viral. This sparked a lot of inquiries about how to tackle the rise of doctored videos. This video spanned twenty seconds and reached Instagram that same week. This video has views above 30,000 and it made Mark the main topic on Twitter for a while. Mark appeared to be addressing CBS news in the video, and though the video had a caption that depicted a talk on measures to protect the elections, the utterances made in the altered video communicated something else. CBS had to demand Facebook remove the video because it depicted their name and trademark in a false and unauthorized video.

An Instagram spokesperson, in a response to technology journalists said the video won't be taken down from the platform until third party verifiers review it and tag it as fake, according to their policy of treatment for every form of disinformation. If tagged false, it will be filtered away from Instagram endorsement pages such as Hashtag pages and Explore.

A barrage of tough criticisms hit Facebook when it declined to remove the manipulated footage of Nancy Pelosi who was depicted as drunk and uttering blurry statements.

The unfortunate after effect is that President Trump found it convincing enough as he shared the footage on his Twitter handle.

Benefits of the Deepfakes

This invention has opened up opportunities in the film industry. A movie shot with an actor that died during the shoot will no longer experience a setback or try to find a lookalike. The Deepfake technology can be used to revive such person by using an existing image of the person and simulate it so it appears like it the deceased still in action. Movies can also be played in various languages by syncing the oral movements of the actors in the movie with the dialogue being spoken in the film and making it look realistic.

Also, in the fashion industry, advertisers can hire the image of a celebrity model for running an advertising campaign. They won't need the presence of the model for the shoot sessions. They can simply get another model with an identical physique and swap faces instead.

According to Sven Charlene, Deepfakes deserve appreciation not crucifixion. Humans tend to believe every information they see on the internet or the media without considering the credibility of their sources. Every content has been taken at face value. We let the media mould our thoughts and shape our beliefs and opinions, even our decisions. We danced to their whim as they influenced our choices.

With the Deepfake highly present among us, people will become more aware of content they are exposed to and learn to improve their evaluative abilities instead of dulling them by taking everything they see hook, line and sinker.

It is also good news for big media brands as well. This is because the awareness of Deepfake will make viewers cautious of what they watch and when this occurs, viewers tend to only rely on the big names in the media because they believe they are more credible. Any media outlet susceptible of false and unverified stories will be the ones to suffer the shift in viewership.

Chapter Five: Criticisms Against Deepfakes

This entails the various oppositions against the Deepfake technology.

Due to the malicious use of the deepfakes app, there is a current debate to know the effect of deepfakes on democracy. This debate has led to many researches being carried out to be able to detect fake media contents before the 2020 USA election.

Pentagon's Darpa claims to have spent several millions on her media forensic research program while other start-ups are on the race to be the voice of truth as the campaign begins ahead of the 2020 election.

Politicians in congress have also asked that deepfake be banned for its malicious use.

However, Robert Chesney, a professor of law at the University of Texas, is of the opinion that deepfake isn't the only way to disrupt politics. An example is the Facebook clip of Nancy Pelosi that showed her drunk and slurring words in public. All the miscreants did to achieve this was to slow down the footage.

Misuse

The engineering of images, audio and video could be a deadly mass-mediated phenomenon. Other forgery means for visual and audio has long time existed before the Deepfake came into the scene but what Deepfake brought with its emergence was "closeness to authenticity".

Impact on Originality

A devastating effect of the Deepfake technology is that it is now hard to know the difference between a real video and a fabricated video. This is the extent to which Deepfake technology has progressed. It now doctors' video to look very authentic and it passes detection from the naked eye. Now with general awareness of such powerful forgery technology, the mass audience will quickly lose trust in visual media content even when they are genuine. They will watch an authentic video and likely suspect it as a Deepfake and vice versa. This could be the order of the day. From trust and credibility to doubt and scepticism.

Reactions from the Web

Internet sites such as Twitter and the likes publicly declared that they intend to erase every Deepfake media content and also hinder the perpetrators from using the platform. There was a chat forum on Discord that was used for publications of forged pornographic video of public figures which was subsequently blocked to prevent further public viewing. Even renowned pornographic site, Pornhub made plans to take similar actions though it is doubtful the ban was executed. In September 2018, popular Search engine, Google, included artificially engineered pornographic content in its list of banned contents.

Deepfake's Contribution to Distortion of Information

Information is power and so is its misuse. Distorting information is the act of deliberately transmitting fabricated and unverified data to an audience for malicious intentions as regards politics, public image and perception. Its menace has been worsened by the advent of social media and the dependence of mainstream news outlets on questionable sources.

Deepfake has emerged as a prime weapon in the fight against true and quality information or content. It's fast placing synthetic media side by side with original content. A survey carried out by ICFJ revealed that an estimate of 71% of practicing journalists harvest their news stories from social media platforms and sadly, only 11% of them take the pains to verify what they get as news-worthy content to determine if it's synthetic or authentic.

Deepfakes keeps deceiving our newsmen. There is the issue of political bots as well. It's a software that generates political write-ups capable of intensifying radical and fanatical views, subduing the voices of the minority via hate speech. Many bots account exist on social media to create propaganda capable of negatively influencing the audience and their choice of candidate.

Social media sites detected this menace, traced it to the existence of numerous bot accounts and deleted a massive number of them in the year 2018. The awareness campaign against the existence of such bots amplified when user guides were written and published on how to spot these bots.

However, the bad news is these bots are getting smarter and more intelligent.

These bots have the ability to speak and may as well manipulate political scenarios. With the added ability of speech, detection and differentiation of bots from human will become increasingly difficult.

Here are hard-core instances of the power or impact of disinformation by the Deepfake in the political scenario. In Myanmar, rumours were generated online about the Muslim Rohingya minority section, these rumours proved lethal as it resulted in mass killings. Thousands of people died. In India, misinformation campaigns led to harassment of females and subsequent assaults on journalists. In Europe, right wing political parties used fabricated stories published online to propagate the agenda of isolation and fear. Such stories centred on the false claim of refugee violence against females.

The video and audio modification ability of Deepfake has made it an important contributor to this present age of disinformation. It is single-handedly responsible for a large chunk of the disinformation that is misleading the global audience. This is so because visual and auditory media content are the primary media content there is.

The speculation to this current trend is that the near future will witness manipulation beyond the visual and auditory senses. Technologies capable of manipulating the other senses will soon emerge taking the level of forgery to a whole new dimension.

Despite the outcry and verbal protests against the use of Deepfakes to distort information online, the menace still powers on. Digital propaganda expert, Sam Willey, proposes strategic responses to combat future deception by these powerful tools of forgery.

Limitations of DeepFake and Learnings

While it is exciting to use the DeepFake technology, there are clear limits on what can be done with this technology:

1. You need several pictures of your
    target. You need minimum of 300
    to 2000 images of a single person
    you would like to use for video to
    help the network learn how to
    recreate the image. The number of
    images you need depends on how
    the faces vary and its close match
    with the original video. This works
    mostly for celebs and political
    figures that have several pictures
    online.

2. You need Training Data that
    Represents the Goal of the Video:
    The images you want to impose
    have to be trained to match the
    facial expressions, orientations as
    well as lighting existing in the

original video. In essence, for an average individual, most of the limited pictures available are usually front-facing like selfies and so this limits the face swap to front facing videos. You can only have varieties when working with pictures of celebs.

3. It is quite expensive to build models: To get a fair result, you would require at least 72 hours at the cost of $0.50 a GPU per hour. It cost approximately $36 to build a model needed to swap one person to another and vice versa. This is minus the bandwidth needed for the training data and the CPU and

I/O for pre-processing. You would need a model for every pair you do.

4. Although it is cheap to run models, it is not free: to swap a video on GPU, it would take about 5 to 20 times the duration of the original video. For example, if you need to generate a 1-minute 1080p video, you would need 18 minutes. With the GPU, you are able to speed up the face detection code and the core model.

5. It cost less time and money when reusing models.

Chapter Six: General Adversarial Networks; Algorithms for Deepfakes

This machine learning network was invented by Ian Goodfellow in the year 2014. He developed a system of two neural networks (the generator and the discriminator) that are sparred against each other like a game contest. This algorithm is the artificial intelligence tool that is used to create Deepfakes.

This method has made Deepfake lethal and feeding this method a particular set of training data enables it to come up with novel data consistent with the same statistics as the source data. Take for instance, an image data trained on the general adversarial networks can enable these algorithms create a new picture that will look genuine on the surface level to observers.

The intention of the generative network algorithm is to amplify the error rates of the discriminative network. These data are cycled between them in a form of distribution.

Back propagation makes these two algorithms become better after each spar. The generator becomes better at creating engineered data that could pass for real while the discriminator gets better at detecting these Deepfakes.

Practical Applications of the General Adversarial Networks

This entails the various areas these algorithms can be used. This enables readers to have an idea of how capable this system is.

Advertising Fashion

These algorithms are capable of engineering images of non-existent fashion models and save advertisers the cost of hiring a real model, photographer, makeup artist and get a studio space. These algorithms are also capable of making campaigns for fashion advertisers. The cost cutting advantage of this has made this invention a welcome novelty in the profession of fashion modelling. Advertisers can spend less capital and maximise profits using these algorithms to create a simulated advertisement.

Gaming

In the year 2018, the general adversarial network was applied in video games. It upgraded the visual quality of games by improving on the 2D resolution quality and reanimating them in 4k resolutions and higher resolutions as well. This was possible via training of imagery and reconstructing to fit the game's resolution. This could also result in sharper, more impressive qualities of the

2D imagery. So, this is the algorithm's version yet traits of the original quality are still retained. Very good instances of this application are Resident Evil, Max Payne and so on.

Misuse of the Algorithm

This powerful technology has been used for bad intentions as well. Producing fake media content that comes as close in quality as the original media content, concerns has been drawn to this development. This neural network is capable of, and has been used to make fake social media profiles that looks real with seemingly realistic photos of people who actually aren't real. These profiles due to the quality of these software appears very convincing.

In May, 2019, the Californian legislature proposed a bill that will prohibit the use of these algorithms to forge or engineer pornographic videos of public figures without their express permission.

Imagine a society where digital security becomes a thing of the past, because an unchecked progress of artificially created media content reaching a level of quality so sublime, that a sizeable portion of the population will be successfully deceived into believing such news. What's worse is that evidence can be fabricated to set up innocent people and get them convicted for crimes they have no idea about.

Even a video clip can be doctored from a single photo of you courtesy Samsung.

Diverse Applications of these Algorithms

The general adversarial network can be used to fabricate seemingly realistic photos that features the properties of a game setting. Putting things such as decor and other handy items in the place so the game scene looks alive.

Its capable of making 3D versions of image subjects and movement patterns from video clips.

It can also be used to change facial appearance in photos to make it seem like the individual in the picture is advancing in age.

This algorithm is capable of predicting or speculating the effect the change in climatic conditions can have on a building over time.

It can transform the image of an individual after picking up the voice of that person through its Speech2Face model.

Chapter Seven: Deepfake Detection; The Only Way Out.

According to Prof. Ira Kemelmacher of the University of Washington, if there is awareness about how the Deepfake technology can develop, then there can surely be a way a counter technology can be developed as well. A technology whose sole purpose of existence will be to detect contents produced by Deepfakes.

The good news is such technology is currently being researched on and developed, though it's still at the cradle stage. The technology design is a learning system with an experimentation with large volumes of data, about 25,000 photos. It is designed to expose Deepfakes in the near future.

Another party in the research field is the United States Military. They are researching on software solutions to fight the menace of Deepfakes. Another player as well, Gfycat, of recent, made a public proclamation stating that they have invented a system hinged on artificial intelligence which is able to expose and obstruct Deepfakes in the years to come. Social Media platform, Facebook also made it known that they intend to use a tool they manufactured to pick up the trails of Deepfake content so that they can then be forwarded to verifiers for manual checking.

The bad news is all the above-mentioned technologies have one common ground; they all need a lot of source material just like the Deepfakes. To fight Deepfake, it has to operate like Deepfake. The source material is vital if these technologies want to build up the important intelligence they need for this fight. This process is time-demanding.

Well, there is still a way to verify contents that are Deepfakes. It is a process made up of multiple steps. This is manual verification. Here, the things to look out for will be stated.

Deepfake Detection Software

Artificial intelligence can also be used to detect Deepfake not only to engineer them. Studies carried out by Professor Siwei Lyu, University of Albany, has revealed that facial exchanges and alternations creates inconsistencies in the resolution of the image which can be picked by algorithms using the technique of deep learning.

Neural networks responsible for the invention of the Deepfake technology, can also be used to recognize flaws across the numerous frames in a video development that is a consequence of face alternations.

A group of scholars from UC Santa Barbara and UC Riverside, has invented methods that will be helpful in recognizing digital tweaks, such as scaling and splicing which is commonly used to produce Deepfakes.

Researchers has been growing in their numbers thanks to the Media Forensics program carried out by DARPA. A program oriented to fight the issue of the Deepfakes. It endorses the manufacturing of technologies for the automatic testing of the authenticity of media content whether it is a photo or video.

This war waged against the Deepfake is a tough one on equal footing because despite how advanced the technologies invented to combat and contain Deepfakes may be, there will always be a challenge for them as Deepfake is advancing too.

Admittedly, the state of the Deepfake verification technologies will not be perfect. It is unfortunate that the most sophisticated authentication method for the Deepfake may not be up to par with the most sophisticated Deepfake generation method.

Another downside to this is that these "solutions" cannot affect the course of anything if it is not utilized. In other words, impact cannot be made in the fight against Deepfakes if these technologies are not utilized.

The interconnectedness of the internet has a propagative nature that makes whatever content is uploaded on it spread across. This means that a Deepfake uploaded on the internet will eventually reach its intended target audience without having to be flagged down by a software that detects Deepfakes.

With the issue of trust for whatever content might be uploaded be it authentic or fake, it will be worsened when there are contrasting judgements on a content (image of video) being real or fabricated. Also, people will be torn between accepting a Deepfake as real due to its believability or accepting the verdict of the software which flags such content as a fake.

Factors to Look Out for in Detecting Deepfakes

The Entire Physical Appearance

You need to carefully look at the content to notice the inconsistency in it. Critically examine if the face sits well on the body. Also, check if the poise aligns with the facial expressions. If the content is a Deepfake, there will surely be something off here. This is because most Deepfakes that are carried out are mostly facial exchanges which despite the time and data taken to make it work, isn't still aligned to the peak of perfection.

Face Glitches

Many Deepfakes give themselves away with this. The faces flicker and they look off. This is because the face is more like a well-worn mask. It is only the face that is swapped. Not the neck nor the hair. So, imagine a strange face trying to align with a different neck or hair, it can be done very well and engineered to look normal but there will always be a loop. Somewhere the face doesn't align with. If you detect this, you are most likely looking at a doctored content.

Duration of the Footage

Though the technology for Deepfakes is automated and done by a software, the deep learning process that comes from analysing large volumes of data is an arduous process. It has been observed that most Deepfake videos just last for a few seconds. So, if during verification, there is no clear reason why the footage is that short, it is an indication of fakery.

Audio Recording

Unless the person is using the Speech2Face app for the audio, the sound can't be modified and therefore, it will not match the face in the image or footage or sound will be absent in the clip. Watch the lip movement closely, if its motion isn't in sync with the sound of the clip, it's most likely a fake

Origin of the Recording

Tracing the first individual or social media account that shared or uploaded such content goes a long way for easy detection of the fake content. You can deduce the context of the video and pick out the details in the first content. Through comparisons drawn between that and the one undergoing verification, you can know which is which.

The Oral Cavity

Deepfakes have only been able to deceive us with faces so far. The details of the video feed are not so easily manipulated like the swapping of faces. In fake videos, you will notice that the person's tongue and teeth tend to appear blurry at some point. Artificial intelligence is yet to learn just how to manipulate this.

Observation of Details in Slow Motion

Play the video you want to verify and set it to play in slow motion. Then observe the details in the clip. Inconsistencies in the video background, as well as changes in the picture can be spotted more easily.

Eyelid Blinking

The average human blink every few seconds. Between the range of 2-8 seconds. Artificial intelligence may have perfected face swapping but they certainly haven't perfected how these faces blink. So, this is another tool to use in detecting Deepfakes.

The above methods are said to be effective to an extent. They won't give 100 percent results. More effective ways are being considered for the detection of the Deepfake. However, there are also software-based solutions coming up as further information on how the Deepfake can be spotted and distinguished from the original content.

Digital Signatures, Deepfake and Oppressive Governments

Digital signature is meant to serve as a trail of originality for content such as video and photos. In Washington, the proposed solution of the digital signature was in trend for a while as it drew considerations. Cameras (Photo, Video and Mobile) are expected to input their signatures digitally on what they capture. This is a way of communicating to viewers that the content they are looking at was physically captured and produced by a real camera and not engineered or fabricated.

Superficially, the idea seemed like a welcome boost in the fight against Deepfakes because of the simplicity and budget-friendly cost of the solution and because it can be quickly and easily incorporated into the existing digital workflow to certify the video is original and communicate same to viewers when they watch it.

The downside to this proposed solution is that although the digital signature may help with the authentication of content, but it also helps surveillance security outfits to easily pinpoint the precise source of the footage capturing police cruelty and depravity.

It must be known that Deepfakes still have a lot of progress to make, and so do not yet generate enough engineered content to make up a sizeable chunk of the available doctored content online.

Digital signature is a solution with many flaws and loop holes. It doesn't authenticate scripted videos where lookalikes are used or genuine locations and properties being used to stage implausible scenes that are difficult to verify, due to the low quality of the mobile phone camera.

An actual video feed of a law enforcer in a dictatorial regime where rule of law and human rights meant nothing, shown beating up an unfortunate demonstrator may be used and mislabelled as proof of police cruelty elsewhere.

It is difficult to get a complete clip when being captured by a mobile phone camera this is because those witnessing the particular incident don't capture it from the onset. They try to gauge how newsworthy such incidents might be and when they actually perceive it to be, they take out their phones and try to capture such an incident when it might have escalated already and when such video is published or uploaded online, it only contains the climax and the conclusive aspect.

This situation applies to documenting of seemingly police cruelty and the video only captures the arrest of an individual and not the preceding sequence of events that led to such arrest. It could be a situation the police were trying to prevent the individual from resisting arrest and may resort to force but the incomplete clip will likely capture this part and portray it to the audience as a classic example of police cruelty.

Such videos can be doctored to promote or combat an oppressive government depending on who is tweaking the controls of the Deepfake software. The video can be edited to show the law enforcement in either a positive or negative light. Now here, the issue at hand is not the authenticity of the clip but the authenticity of the narrative i.e. how the footage was captured and portrayed. Inputting digital signatures into such videos does nothing to verify its authenticity if the narrative was biased and probably false.

Still the solution of digital signatures may not do anything to address the issue of the Deepfake. This is due to the mass availability of phones and cameras and the fact that not every gadget user can meet up with upgrades yearly so even if digital signatures are provided by these gadget manufacturers, it does little or nothing to stem the tide of artificial intelligence-manipulated content.

It is feared that in the new future the solution of digital signatures may not hold water anymore as hackers are working hard to manipulate the signing of captured content by devices, so the resultant effect will be the input of digital signatures in photos and videos by any computer system, and the input of false content into the camera's network of electronic circuits, enabling the host device of that camera to sign it itself therefore endorsing falsified content to be authentic.

Anyways, even at this unpleasant revelation, the bright side is the technical dexterity required to successfully input digital signatures into falsified content is only possessed by a handful of people.

Not many people can reverse engineer digital signatures as it isn't a simple process. So, they may still be partially easy to spot because there is a small number of devices signing their content.

If Governments were to be the producers of the Deepfakes, it would still herald political instability in the country as political opponents will be the victims of fabricated propaganda.

The guaranteed end digital signature could put to the menace of the Deepfakes will be an inaccessible digital signature system but then the ramifications of such possibility is farfetched.

If you get a plastic lens attached to a phone camera, and position it to face the screen of another phone or a computer screen, you can capture the video clip being played on the device it is facing, and it will appear as if you are recording live but is a falsified content. The accurate spacing and configuration of the lens will capture the video being played and the content captured will be infused with the phone's digital signature to authenticate it as a real content. So even the solution of the digital signature can be circumvented.

So, with this technique which is as simple as reverse engineering digital signatures is complex, the means to override digital signatures as a means of detecting Deepfakes is now available to any user of a smartphone. For a dictatorial and oppressive government, this is a favourable development because they can now easily track down activists and individuals involved in citizen journalism.

For a while, colour printers have been inputting a signage on every page they print out, it is a Machine Identification Code also known as "Yellow dots". Such signage is in the form of a concealed code that is veiled from the ordinary eye on the top of every printed page, but it can be quickly and easily unveiled on behalf of security agents in their quest to find out the exact printer that the page came out from.

The same thing applies to cameras for photos and videos making the solution of digital signatures a reverse problem, because making the input of digital signatures mandatory for every digital or electronic device that can capture video and pictures can make whatever content easily traced back to its original owner i.e. the original owner of the device that captured such content. Therefore, it will be very easy for oppressive governments to quell opposition and the activities of dissidents.

Any content that paints or portrays these repressive governments in an unpleasant light will be scouted for, traced to the home device and have the owner arrested by security agents of the governments. It can be used either ways though. Take for instance, a video recorded discreetly of a government official accepting a bribe to perform its duty can be used either way; to identify and arrest such official for corruption, or trace the person who recorded the video and arrest or eliminate the individual.

Social media as a platform for publication or uploading of visual media content, removes digital signage from every content that is on it but even then, their vast network of cloud systems will surely contain trails of the original content, which of course will have the digital signage which means anonymous publication on social media platform can still be traced.

Every photo has response traits that has its origins tied to the camera sensor which took the shot, in essence, an image can be tracked down to the camera's sensor due to the tiny flaws and varieties in the production of each sensor. However, this is limited to verifying that a particular content came from a recognized device. It doesn't extend to tracing the content uploaded, to the exact device that captured it.

A technique to salvage the digital signature circumvention is the bulk issuance of digital signage for devices i.e. issuing a certain digital signage for a large number of devices, instead of a unique signage to each device. This technique can make rebels of a bad government get away with uploading contents anonymously, and without fear of it being tracked back to them. Trying to identify such digital signage and trace it to a certain device will give you an option of a large number of devices, leaving you completely uncertain of the particular one that uploaded the video or image.

But then the flaw of this technique is that it isn't fool proof, because it takes just a single compromised device to wreck the whole anonymity of the technique.

Generators of the Deepfake content can input digital signage on their fabricated content through the aid of "cryptographic digital signage on camera" making the content look like it isn't coming from a software, but a camera and thereby giving it authenticity and making detection of its fakery nearly impossible.

So, in conclusion, digital signatures are perceived as a complicated solution to the menace of the Deepfake and a welcome boost for oppressive governments using their security outfits to neutralise every form of media-oriented opposition with relative ease.

Legal Landscape for the Deepfake

When it comes to the Deepfake, the legal framework is anything but simple. These are structures that can be possibly affirmed to battle Deepfakes, they include; copyright, publicity right, section 43, sub section A of the Lanham act, defamation torts, false portrayal, deliberate affliction of emotional duress. The other side contains the insurances bestowed by the First Amendment and the Fair Use doctrine in the law of copyright, as well as section 230 of the Communications Decency Act, which makes provisions for social media platforms and any web page that welcomes third party content.

It will indeed be tough for the judicial system to find its footing. Protection provided by court rulings bestowed on the subjects or victims of the Deepfake risk being on bad terms with the First Amendment and such rulings could be put in a position where they are tied down by appeal.

The point here is that there will be no buoyant measure to battle the menace of the Deepfakes if the court rulings ensuring the victims of the Deepfakes is inadequate. Saying the consequence of this can be detrimental is an understatement. Deepfakes will continue to thrive with no stringent legislative panacea for it.

Measures to lessen the stated provisions of section 230 of the Community Decency Act for the intention of facing the threat the Deepfake is overtly being, will cause chaos and untold effects on the ecosystem of the internet. While this uncertainty plays out in the court house, two deductions can be confidently made; there is an available body of legislative provisions that can battle the Deepfakes and calling these legislative provisions inadequate is a hurried decision.

Recent potential legislations have been brought forward by legislators at the state and federal level as their response to being pressured to make something happen as regards the issue of fighting the Deepfake. Easier requested for than done, the truth is it will be tough to constitute a legislation whose sale emphasis is on the Deepfake without clashing with the First Amendment Act and being verbose to laws already in place.

In December, 2018, a now obsolete senate bill was brought forward, it criminalised "using any means or facility of interstate or foreign commerce" to "create with the intent to distribute, a Deepfake with the intent that the distribution of the Deepfake would facilitate criminal or tortuous conduct under federal, state, local or tribal law" such was the provision of the bill as exactly stated.

The New York state legislative officials have contemplated a bill that will ban specific uses of a person's replica or clone created digitally and uphold one's publicity right which endorses the privacy of one's persona whether the individual is alive or dead. As expected, this didn't go down well with the entertainment industry. A known response from the industry was a letter from the vice president of the Walt Disney company which summarises that, adopting the bill will interfere with the activities of the film makers to tell fictional stories based on true individuals and incidents. The letter also stated that there is a public interest in these stories and those who make or tell these stories are insured by the First Amendment Act.

Chapter Eight: Final Remarks on the Deepfake

The bottom line is no matter how advanced the detection equipment for the Deepfake becomes, they won't push the Deepfakes out of existence.

Furthermore, no matter how specific to detail and adequate legislative provisions might be as regards the Deepfake, it can only be effective in facing the possible damage that can be wrecked by the Deepfake, especially considering the short span of time required to make, upload or publish, and transmit or distribute digital media content.

Intensified public sensitisation may help fight the issue of the Deepfake. Information they should know will be helpful to them. They should be aware that the sighting of glitches or flickers in a video isn't automatic evidence that a video is fabricated or engineered. If a Deepfake of very good quality has been uploaded on the internet, it will only take a short period of time for credible evidence to surface, more likely another video to disprove the quality of the Deepfake. This definitely won't erase the Deepfake from existence but it will help cripple the negative effect.

www.ingramcontent.com/pod-product-compliance
Lightning Source LLC
Chambersburg PA
CBHW031221050326
40689CB00009B/1424